THE HERITAGE COLLECTION

Queen Nandi

Rosemond Sarpong Owens

Illustrator: Amina Yaqoob

Queen Nandi

Copyright © 2021 by Rosemond Sarpong Owens

Illustrator: Amina Yaqoob

Library of Congress Control Number - 2021911209

All rights reserved.

No part of this publication may be reproduced, stored in a retrieval system, a database and/or published in any form or by any means, electronic, mechanical, photocopying, recording or otherwise, without the prior written permission of the publisher.

Published by Lion's Historian Press
https://www.lionshistorian.net/

CONTENTS

CHAPTER ONE: NANDI'S BIRTH 1

CHAPTER TWO: THE EARLY YEARS 3

CHAPTER THREE: MAJOR LIFE CHANGES 5

CHAPTER FOUR: THE BIRTH OF SHAKA & MARRIAGE 7

CHAPTER FIVE: REJECTION 9

CHAPTER SIX: A WELCOMING PLACE 11

CHAPTER SEVEN: RESILIENCE 13

CHAPTER EIGHT: QUEEN MOTHER 15

CHAPTER NINE: QUEEN NANDI'S DEATH 17

CHAPTER TEN: REVERED MEMORY 19

REFERENCES 21

ACKNOWLEDGEMENTS 22

AUTHOR'S NOTE 23

ABOUT AUTHOR 24

QUEEN NANDI EDITORIAL REVIEW 25

PLEASE LEAVE A REVIEW 26

OTHER BOOKS IN THE HERITAGE COLLECTION 27

DEDICATION

To the students at the

Molo Mhlaba Girls Schools

CHAPTER ONE: NANDI'S BIRTH

Many, many years before Europeans settled in present day South Africa, Zulus lived in the southeastern part of Africa.

The Zulu people are one of many tribes living in South Africa. Amongst the Zulus are different clans who farm and hunt for a living.

Zulus from the Langeni clan lived on green lush land good for raising cattle and growing crops. The Langeni ruler or chief called Bhebhe lived in a village called Melmoth. Today, Melmoth is a small town, considered the gateway to the Zulu highlands.

In 1760, Chief Bhebhe welcomed a beautiful daughter he named Ndlovukazi Nandi kaBebe eLangeni, meaning *The Sweet One*. I bet no one imagined what lay ahead of her. We will find out!

CHAPTER TWO: THE EARLY YEARS

Nandi and three sisters — Mkabayi, Mmama and Nomawa — grew up on a Kraal in Melmoth. The Kraal is an enclosed settlement surrounded by a circle of huts where families lived. The girls enjoyed playing in the fields, while caring for the family's livestock outside the Kraal.

Although Nandi lived in the chief's home, the household did not treat her as royalty. Nandi learned trading, just like clan members. She traded from city to city, traveling with the caravan, making Nandi confident and strong.

CHAPTER THREE: MAJOR LIFE CHANGES

Nandi travelled with a caravan to trade. After trading, she visited family in Babanango, a small village about 36 miles from Melmoth. Nandi's life would never be the same again.

The caravan she travelled with ran into a group of Zulu warriors. Among them was Senzangakhona, son of the Zulu King. Senzangakhona and Nandi grew close and she became pregnant with his child.

The Langeni clan sent a message to the Zulu King that he was going to be a grandfather. The King and his family rejected the messenger and message. They mocked Nandi, claiming her enlarged waistline was due to illness caused by a bite from the Shaka beetle.

Nandi's family claimed damages from the King. Nandi was pregnant and unmarried, then a disgrace to her family. Nandi participated in the discussion, defending her honor with a demand for a herd of fifty-five cattle. The Zulus must pay a price for the hurt done to her. Senzangakona's people delivered the herd to Nandi, her bravery paid off.

CHAPTER FOUR: THE BIRTH OF SHAKA & MARRIAGE

Nandi gave birth to her son in 1787 and named him Shaka, after the beetle to spite Senzangakhona. She also gave a nickname *Umlilwana*, meaning, *Little Blazing Fire*. Nandi kept this name just between the two of them.

After the birth, Nandi and newborn Shaka travelled to the Zulu capital to meet with the King. Senzangakhona agreed to marry Nandi. She moved into his kraal with her son, as his third wife.

Nandi's family disapproved of her marriage because Nandi's mother and the Zulu King were descendants from the same family. Things were not going well for Nandi. Poor Nandi.

CHAPTER FIVE: REJECTION

Nandi and Shaka did not feel welcome in Senzangakhona's home. They were constantly bullied by Senzangakhona's other wives and children. Nandi suffered great humiliation, rejection, and insults.

On the other hand, Langeni women teased and embarrassed Nandi through poems and songs. When Nandi saw that her people also rejected her, she knew her situation had to change for the better. She must take action for her son's sake.

CHAPTER SIX: A WELCOMING PLACE

Nandi wished for a better life, leaving Senzangakhona's home. She moved from place to place, looking for a safe settlement.

Nandi and Shaka stayed with the Qwabe people, where she met Gendeyana. Nandi married Gendeyana and produced a son, Ngwadi. Yet, Nandi remained unhappy and moved again.

Nandi and sons joined the Mthethwa people ruled by Dingiswayo. The Mthethwa people welcomed Nandi, providing a safe refuge for her sons, Shaka and Ngwadi. Nandi also gave birth to a daughter, Nomcoba, when she joined the Mthethwa people. Nandi's children flourished.

Chief Dingiswayo noticed Shaka's good skills with the Zulu stick. Shaka won each fight with the boys in the settlement. Chief Dingiswayo took Shaka under his wing, teaching him how to fight. Shaka became a warrior and leader, and later joined Dingiswayo's army.

CHAPTER SEVEN: RESILIENCE

Nandi loved and cared for her children. She travelled long distances to provide food. Nandi made life-changing decisions, moving her children to a good place for development. She endured many hardships but bounced back each time.

Nandi became resilient, determined to help her children succeed. Nandi developed a strong bond with her firstborn. Nandi taught Shaka about his Zulu people, destiny as a leader and the power of unity. Shaka in turn loved and revered his mother.

CHAPTER EIGHT: QUEEN MOTHER

After Shaka's father Senzangakhona died around 1815, Shaka took the Zulu throne. He appointed Nandi, Queen mother, advisor to King Shaka. Queen Nandi's sound counsel helped King Shaka to avoid unnecessary wars.

Queen Nandi took charge of state affairs, ensuring that it ran smoothly while King Shaka secured the kingdom's boundaries. Then Zulu women managed households while the men took care of fighting. However, Queen Nandi trained Zulu women in governance. They took charge of the military on the home front while King Shaka travelled.

To honor Queen Nandi, King Shaka established an all-female regiment that often fought in the front lines of his army. This was a new thing in those days.

CHAPTER NINE: QUEEN NANDI'S DEATH

On October 10, 1827, Queen Nandi Bhebhe died after an illness. It was a sad day for the Zulu people. For King Shaka, his world came to a crushing end. Queen Nandi was his counselor and support. He knew that without his mother, he would have failed many times as a King. He wondered how his life could go on without his mother. The grief was unbearable.

CHAPTER TEN: REVERED MEMORY

Historians refer to King Shaka as the greatest Zulu King. King Shaka extended the kingdom's boundaries and increased prosperity. He taught war strategy and helped Zulus defeat many enemies. Queen Nandi's influence on Shaka's life helped to shape his destiny. When a hurt and humiliated Nandi nicknamed her firstborn, *Little Blazing Fire*, she placed his life on a certain path. Mothers know best!

Queen Nandi also broke the glass ceiling. Throughout history, a man usually holds the job of king or ruler. However, Queen Nandi demonstrated women might successfully rule kingdoms also. Nandi rose above adversity to become a powerful queen mother. She never gave up on life or her son. Today, Queen Nandi's life teaches women around the world resilience.

On February 20, 2018, King Goodwill Zweilthini officially renamed a regional hospital in honor of Queen Nandi. *Queen Nandi Regional Hospital* is in Empangeni, about thirty-two miles from Melmoth. A befitting memorial for a woman who inspired others to strive past adverse situations and not to settle for less!

REFERENCES

- Lipschutz, Mark R., and R. Kent Rasmussen. *Dictionary of African Historical Biography*. 2nd ed. Berkeley, CA: University of California Press, 1986.

- *"Queen Nandi-1760-1827"* Encyclopedia.com, https://www.encyclopedia.com/women/encyclopedias-almanacs-transcripts-and-maps/nandi-c-1760s-1827

- Shamase, Maxwell D., *"The royal women of the Zulu monarchy through the keyhole of oral history: Queens Nandi (c. 1764 – c.1827) and Monase (c. 1797 – 1880)"* Inkansiyo: Journal of Humanities and Social Sciences, Vol. 6 No. 1 (2014)

- *"History of Queen Nandi Regional Hospital"*, Retrieved from http://www.kznhealth.gov.za/QueenNandi/history.htm

ACKNOWLEDGEMENTS

For her work on and support of this book, thanks to Marjy Marj, (Marjorie Boafo Appiah).

For guiding the manuscript through the copyediting phase, thanks to Letitia deGraft Okyere.

For his tireless efforts at formatting and design, thanks to Nasim Malik Sarkar.

AUTHOR'S NOTE

Growing up, I didn't own books. Thankfully, I had the opportunity to read at the library. A few years ago, I was introduced to Books for Africa, a nonprofit that ships books to children in Africa. Thanks to their efforts, several children in indigenous areas now have access to books. Please learn about the Books for Africa initiative and their mission to end the book famine in Africa.

BOOKS FOR AFRICA

Books For Africa is the world's largest shipper of books to Africa, shipping over 50 million hard-copy and over 3 million digital books to Africa since 1988.

For more information about Books For Africa, including how to donate books or funds, please visit www.booksforafrica.org.

ABOUT AUTHOR

Rosemond Sarpong Owens is a diversity, equity & inclusion professional. She has a passion for history and storytelling and is inspired to share stories of heroes and heroines of African descent. Sarpong Owens is a wife and mother to three girls who love to read. She hopes that this book encourages children to be proud of themselves and their heritage.

QUEEN NANDI EDITORIAL REVIEW

The story of Queen Nandi as a leader in her own right has been neglected in the annals of history. Most people know her as the mother of one of the greatest leaders of the Zulu nation but how does a woman raise such a remarkable man unless she too is a force to be reckoned with?

Rosemond Sarpong Owens pays tribute to this remarkable woman in her children's book: Queen Nandi. By writing this book specifically for children, the future generations of African children and those around the world, Rosemond memorializes the story of African women and the leadership roles they played in nation building throughout history. Queen Nandi's story is also a reminder of women's resilience in the face of unmentionable patriarchal systems of exclusion and oppression. Young African girls and children are very fortunate to be reading Rosemond's work on women, particularly Queen Nandi. Womandla to the world!

Rethabile Mashale Sonibare
Co-founder & Director at Molo Mhlaba Schools

PLEASE LEAVE A REVIEW

Please take a moment to rate and review Queen Nandi as this helps others (kids, parents, teachers) discover her story. I love hearing from my readers.

Thank You!

OTHER BOOKS IN THE HERITAGE COLLECTION

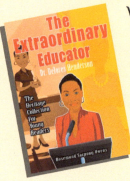

Who is Delores Henderson? A little girl with a love for reading and learning grew up to fight racism to become recognized as the first Black National Distinguished Principal for the state of Minnesota. She blazed the trails and showed us all what is possible if we believe. Readers will learn about her persistence and hard work and be inspired by Delores' indomitable spirit.

The story of Yaa Asantewaa is one of courage and the survival of a kingdom and its people. As a brave warrior, she motivated her people to defend themselves in the fight against British colonialism. Today many parents name their children in her honor.

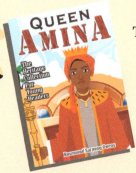

The story of Queen Amina is an important one for girls everywhere. Explore how Queen Amina gained a reputation as a fearless warrior, breaking barriers at a time when men dominated most aspects of life. Queen Amina's life will inspire and encourage you to be fearless.

CPSIA information can be obtained
at www.ICGtesting.com
Printed in the USA
BVHW020836280721
612609BV00003B/2